CHOOSE WISELY

10 Steps to find the
RIGHT financial advisor FOR YOU!

BY
ELIOT DYLAN MARR

Choose Wisely
10 Steps to find the RIGHT financial advisor FOR YOU!
by Eliot Dylan Marr

Printed in the United States of America

ISBN 9781498416368

www.xulonpress.com

INTRODUCTION

I have been truly blessed to help people plan their financial futures; it is something for which I have a passion. In gratitude, I have written this book to give back to the investing community. In this book you will find information to which you may otherwise not be privileged.

My hope and intention is that these ten tips will serve as a guideline to finding the perfect financial advisor for you and your family. Whomever you select to invest with will inevitably make a major difference in the rest of your life, which is why I provide insider information that is extremely important for everyone to know.

This book is intended to be of use to the first time investor with $10,000 to start as well as the tenured investor with $10,000,000. The concepts of this book do not change regarding the amount of assets you have.

I took some complex matters and wrote them in an easy-to-read format to ensure that you fully understand these ten important tips you should follow when choosing a financial advisor.

If you find the information in this book helpful, feel free to pass it along to someone else who could use it. As I mentioned, this book is a "Give-Back," my way of saying thank you for those that allow me to do what I do. It has been a pleasure to be of service to you, and I will continue to work diligently for those who seek my counsel.

Eliot Dylan Marr

TABLE OF CONTENTS

Chapter 1

THE POWER OF A REFERRAL

I Love a Good Steak

Last year my wife and I were traveling, as we tend to do, and I was in the mood for a steak. Not just any steak: an excellent, succulent, red-on-the-inside steak with phenomenal side dishes and a good wine. I went online and found a restaurant chain that we knew and liked, so I made reservations to dine there. Before dinnertime however, I had a conversation with another guest at the hotel where we were staying. During the course of conversation, I mentioned to him that I was craving a good steak, and I told him where we would be dining. He gave me a look of exasperation and said, "Listen, if you want the best steak in this town, you have to go to Steak Heaven. They make their own wine, and their steak can't be beat. My wife and I love it there."

Allow me to break down this referral for you:

He started off with "Listen". People accustomed to being heard love to start fact-stating sentences with that word. It wasn't as if I was checking my stock portfolio as we were talking and hardly paying him any attention. We were both looking at one another, standing and conversing. He said "Listen" because he knew what he was about to say was important to where our conversation was headed.

Then he said, "If you want the best steak in this town..." Of course, I did. The chain restaurant that I had mentioned is a higher-end chain, so I think it was obvious that I desired the best steak in town. The man now had my full attention.

"You have to go to Steak Heaven." He didn't say "Maybe you should try" or "I have heard". He said, "You have to go to..." He said it with a certainty that made me feel that if we did not go where he recommended, we would not be eating the best steak in town.

He followed up by telling me of his own personal experience with Steak Heaven: "They make their own wine." To go to a restaurant where they make their own wine is a bonus, if only because you can bring a new story to your friends back home. I was happy to be having this conversation.

Then he said, "Their steak can't be beat." Period. It could probably have been said more eloquently but certainly not as confidently. In other words, he was saying to me, "If you are like me and like the best, this place will exceed your expectation. You will not find a better steak in this town."

In just a few words, he then summed up the outcome of his personal experience there: "My wife and I love it there." There I was, looking for a place to eat with my wife, and he was telling me that he went there with his wife–and they had a marvelous experience.

Where do you think my wife and I had dinner? If you guessed Steak Heaven, you understand the power of a referral.

A Solid Referral

There is no better and truer form of marketing than when a peer recommends a service or a company. My wife and I went to Steak Heaven instead of a restaurant that we already knew that we liked, because another guest in our hotel had tried Steak Heaven and enjoyed it so much that, although we had just met, he dared to breach polite conversational protocol and pretty much told me what to do.

When you are deciding to select the right financial advisor, you would save yourself a lot of time and possible heartache in the future if you could get a solid referral by a peer. A referral from someone who has done what you are about to do is powerful. It is typically given because there has been evidence of a successful relationship, whether from the person himself or from someone else he knows and trusts. A referral is a valid indicator of what type of experience you could expect. It will always be more valuable than any television commercial, newspaper ad, Google search rank, or catchy jingle. It is the honest manifestation of a person's experience with the service provider.

When a peer gives you a recommendation, he or she understands that you will most likely see him or her again. He will not recommend that your time, energy, and money be spent anywhere if he doesn't feel, in his heart, that it would not be beneficial to you. This individual knows for certain if his referral took his calls, ran his practice as advertised, called back, and if he was informative, knowledgeable and pleasant to work with. It is as if he is willing to put his word on the line, his reputation on the line. He knows if it doesn't work out for you, you will not consult with him again in these types of matters. Ever.

I assume that you do not want to be the reason why someone went through a bad experience. I know that when I recommend someone for a particular service, I only do it when I have concrete knowledge that the service provider would be able to perform at a high level. A referral is the best place to start when selecting anything, especially a financial advisor.

Birds of a Feather

At the risk of crossing the politically correct barrier, not every family brings home the same paycheck. There are people with higher tax brackets than others. There are different classes. What a friend of yours might think is the absolute best might be different than what you think is the absolute best. It's not that either of you are lying. It's that your life experiences are different, because perhaps you have been able to experience a higher quality of life, in terms of materialistic possessions, than your friend. This is why I say that not all referrals are the same, and it has nothing to do with how honest the person is.

The fact that the person who referred us to the restaurant was also a guest at the hotel where we were staying gave him a level of credibility. We were both staying at the finest hotel in the city. I felt that his taste would be closer to mine, than say, a good friend of mine who lives in a one-bedroom studio apartment with his wife and two children. I say this not to demean anyone but to make a point: it is as important to take into account the referrer as the actual referral.

It stands to reason that a person in a similar situation to yours has searched for the same services. If someone's net worth mirrors yours in terms of assets, investments, goals, and even age, whomever he recommends as a Financial Advisor should be placed at the highest end of your to-call list.

Another person to trust to refer you a sound financial advisor would be your CPA. CPAs are profoundly familiar with their clients' investments, financial situations, and any personal tax issues they might have. They most likely have other clients who have been in the same situation as you and have seen what a good financial advisor did for them. They can be instrumental in steering you in the right direction with a credible referral for a financial advisor.

Chapter Recap:

- No other form of marketing is better than a referral. ("Their steak can't be beat!")

- A referral is the most trusted method of being introduced to a financial advisor

- Peer recommendations trump recommendations from friends.

Chapter 2

OPTIONS EQUALS DIVERSIFICATION

I n life, and I believe most people would agree, having options is a good thing. We start off every day with the power of choice. Those decisions trail into our past, create our present and map out our future. Amid the rampant flow of information, we are beset by options like never before. The choice is no longer Coke or Pepsi, McDonalds or Burger King, or NBC, ABC, or CBS. Marketers have brilliantly found ways to get their products in front of us to the point that, for someone making a purchase, research is sometimes required. I dare say this is not a bad thing. I would much rather have options and be able to find a product that suits my specific need than be stuck with something that doesn't do everything I want.

As I mentioned before, my wife and I enjoy traveling. Selecting the right vacation place at times, though, is a process. Here is how it is at times at my house:

"Oh look honey, there is a jazz club right down the street from the hotel we would stay at, plus we can swim with the dolphins if we go to Bermuda. What do you think?" she'll ask. She knows I love a good live jazz band, and I know dolphins have always fascinated her. She was researching the perfect place for us to go so we could both do what we liked.

"That sounds good. I remember you saying that you always wanted to swim with dolphins. Let's book it," I'll answer.

"You are just the most handsome, caring, incredibly talented, most awesome man in the world," she will say. It's actually something she says often.

Okay, maybe she has never said that, but the point is she easily found information that gave us good options for things to do on our upcoming vacation. By selecting the right choices, you enhance your quality of life. Seemingly good options and good deals tend to be everywhere: where to eat dinner, what movie to see, which television series to get hooked on, and so on and so forth.

Have you gone shopping for a new car lately? Talk about options! Convertible or hard top, Italian leather seats or cloth, chrome rims or alloy rims, Ferrari fire engine red or pearl of essence, dual children LCD entertainment system with wireless headphones or compatible ports for iPods... The choices are extensive. However, every one of these options, when chosen correctly, combines to customize a vehicle that is absolutely perfect for you, your lifestyle, and your family. A car that is designed to meet your performance goals can be a costly investment, but every time you drive, it will give you the utmost personal satisfaction to know that this car was built specifically to meet your goals. When options produce results, you win.

In the world of finances, options equal diversification. Just like being able to select a product to suit your specific tastes, lifestyle and needs, a well-diversified investment portfolio is designed to help you work toward your investment goals. Each product or program that you choose will typically yield you a different result. Investments also produce at different rates, even at different times. I believe it is imperative for someone to have a financial advisor who understands all of the different options available to you in order for you to pursue your goals.

When it comes to the wonderful world of investing, all investment advisors would agree that diversification is a must. There is no magic bullet when it comes to successful investing. It doesn't exist. It's a myth; it hangs out with Bigfoot, Old Nelly and the Chupacabra. Diversifying your portfolio should always be on the top of your list when planning your future. (There is no guarantee that a diversified portfolio will enhance overall returns or outperform a non-diversified portfolio: diversification does not protect against market risks.)

Do not keep all your eggs in one basket. Have you ever heard that old phrase? Of course you have. Phrases like that pass from generation to generation. There is a reason why we know it and why our children know it. It's still a very good idea that has proven to be sound and true.

A well-diversified portfolio can contain a variety of investment vehicles: stocks, bonds, ETFs, annuities, senior secured notes, and a host of different alternative investments. Depending on your personal investment goals, some or all of these might be appropriate for you.

The main thing to understand is that good options are the way to having a well-planned and diversified portfolio.

The caveat to all of this is that, unfortunately, not every Financial Advisor has the breadth of knowledge, nor the appropriate licenses to ensure that all your eggs are in the right baskets. Although options are great, they can tend to make matters a bit convoluted. As a general rule of thumb, a way to make the world of financial investing less confusing is to look for an advisor who can intelligently relay information to eliminate the guesswork.

I would look for an advisor that has the following registrations: Series 7; Series 66; and a State Health, Life and Variable Annuity. I would also recommend that the advisor be an accredited RIA (a Registered Investment Advisor). An advisor with these registrations typically will be able to provide you with all of the investment pieces needed for a dynamic and well-diversified portfolio.

Chapter Recap

- Options equal diversification; your portfolio should be diverse.

- Investing does not require magic, it requires well thought out and carefully planned execution.

Chapter 3

ALPHABET SOUP

H ave you ever looked at the business card of a Financial
Advisor and seen the myriad of different accreditations we have? CFP®, ChFC®, RIA, AAMS®, ADPA®,
AWMA®, ABCDEFG and more… It's quite confusing,
isn't it?

I certainly recommend that you find out what those
acronyms mean. It can definitely be beneficial in the hunt
for your ideal advisor. A couple of great resources are the
websites for the institutions that offer these designations.
The websites for the College for Financial Planning®
(www.cffpinfo.com) and The American College for
Financial Services (www.theamericancollege.edu) are
very informative. Both of these sites could help clear up a
lot of confusion. These sites give a complete description
of course content on all of their designations. I suggest

visiting them and familiarizing yourself with the areas of specialty, especially ones that are aligned with your goals.

The first thing to know about accreditations is they indicate that the professional has comprehensive knowledge in this area. It has been my experience that advisors who go the extra mile to achieve these accolades generally have a passion for or enjoy working with their clients in these areas. I don't know about you, but I want to work with someone who is passionate about what they do. (As a rule of thumb, passionate people are successful in their fields.) Let us take a look at some examples of designations, not necessarily to give you a recommendation but to show you instead the wide variety of areas of specialty.

If you are one of the 76 million baby boomers moving into your retirement years, you are most likely looking for an advisor to assist in your pre- and post-retirement needs. The areas of concern for a retiree or pre-retiree can be vast, and they truly need to be addressed. Most in this age group share the same questions and concerns. The questions range from:

- When can my spouse and I retire?

- How should I manage my assets in retirement?

- What are the best sources of income?

- How will my income taxes be affected in retirement?

- How should I plan my estate?

- How do I plan for possible incapacity?

A CRPC® (Chartered Retirement Planning Counselor) is a designation that specifically addresses these areas. An advisor who has earned this designation has demonstrated a competent understanding in these areas and could be a good resource for a retiree or pre-retiree.

In today's ever-changing society, we see that domestic partnerships are rapidly increasing in popularity. These partnerships are not just found in the LGBT communities but are also becoming quite common among heterosexual couples who have chosen not to marry. These relationships can have very unique financial planning needs and are subject to constantly changing legislation, both at the state and federal levels.

Domestic partnership can involve factors and situations that cause the appropriate financial planning to differ from planning for legally married spouses. An advisor might need to use alternative planning solutions for wealth transfer, taxation, retirement planning and estate planning. A financial advisor with an ADPA® (an Accredited Domestic Partnership Advisor℠) has studied such topics as: wealth transfers for domestic partners; federal taxation issues for domestic partners; retirement planning & retirement issues for domestic partners; and planning for financial, medical, & end-of-life needs of domestic partners.

I would be remiss if I did not discuss two very specific types of designations that can be beneficial for individuals with certain specific needs. The two most respected designations in my industry are the CFP® (Certified Financial Planner) and the ChFC® (Chartered Financial Consultant). They can assist individuals, professionals and small business owners with a variety of advanced financial planning needs. They are knowledgeable in financial planning disciplines including insurance, income taxation, retirement planning, investments and estate planning. These financial advisors are typically very knowledgeable, able to help their clients in most any areas of their financial needs. They have reached the summit of education in our field.

The main thing is not to drown in the alphabet soup. It is important that you do a little research on your own to understand what all of the letters after the name mean.

Once you do, you will become better equipped to pick an advisor who has the skill sets that match your specific goals.

Chapter Recap

- **Don't drown in the Alphabet Soup. Understand what the letters mean after the name.**

- **There are designations which specialize in niche markets**

Chapter 4

COMMUNICATION IS KEY

There are quarterbacks in the NFL, and there is Peyton Manning. In 2013 he played only his second season with the Denver Broncos, and their offense was one of the best in the history of the NFL. There are great chefs, and there is Chef Gordon Ramsay: the Scottish celebrity chef, restaurateur and television personality. There are NBA coaches, and there is Phil Jackson, winner of 11 NBA championships.

What is it about them? Why have they risen to the tops of their professions? The answer is obvious. They know how to communicate!

Manning, a five-time MVP with two different teams, not only communicates like a coach on the field, he is also the most sought after pitchman in the NFL. I'd dare say if the NFL were to ever need just one spokesperson, Mr. Manning would be on top of the list.

Chef Ramsay communicates in an altogether different style, yet he is every bit as effective. His course language has made his shows into must-see TV. Phil Jackson (otherwise known as the Zen Master) managed the massive egos of superstars like Michael Jordan, Kobe Bryant and Shaquille O'Neal. He even took out-of-control rebel Dennis Rodman and, at least during the years he coached him, Rodman behaved like a professional athlete.

These three men understand that communication is key in their professions. They communicate in totally different styles, but their messages are received clearly. At the end of the day, that's all that matters.

It is important for you to understand that not all financial advisors are created equal. While many of us possess the same licenses, there can be big differences in our bedside manner, in the way we communicate with our clients. I have, on occasion, witnessed advisors on the phone with their clients, and I swear the person on the other end of the phone only had time to say *hello, okay* and *goodbye*. Some advisors make sure to ask all the right questions so as to understand the client and his needs. Life happens however: situations arise, and things change. A good advisor will continue to ask the right questions and build a rapport with you so that you are involved in every conversation and never feel hesitant to ask questions. You might luck out and get referred to a great advisor, but if you need to shop around blindly, study the advisor. If he or she tends to dominate the conversations early on, the less control you will feel you have regarding your decisions. Your financial advisor needs to always act like your advisor, and not as if you are just one of his clients. There is a big difference.

Regardless of the knowledge a financial advisor has, if it is not communicated so that the client can comprehend everything, the client will not enjoy that relationship. No one likes to be in a conversation that is above their level of understanding, over-their-head. Oftentimes, people will not let advisors know when they have no idea what was just said. They will just nod and smile and wait for the advisor to say something that they understand, so they can jump back into the conversation. You don't want that type of relationship with your advisor, do you?

If you select a financial advisor who does not communicate effectively, does not transfer relevant information in a timely manner, or makes you feel as if he is speaking in his own language, how will you know that your money is indeed in the right place, or that your retirement funds are where they need to be?

Chapter Recap

- Make sure your advisor communicates with you on a level you are comfortable with.

- Consider picking an advisor who listens as well as speaks.

Chapter 5
THE PROCESS

Every good financial advisor has a process that he or she uses with clients. This process includes not only the initial meeting and the following meetings with recommendations but also how this advisor will work with clients throughout the course of the year. Most advisors have a similar process at the beginning of the relationships, but their structures can vary greatly in how the relationships are maintained and managed year after year. It is important that your advisor set the expectations for your relationship and thoroughly explain exactly how he will service you and your accounts.

Here is an inside look at the very successful process I use with my clients, how I deliver service to them throughout the year.

My process starts with the telephone. I introduce myself to my potential clients and see what they are needing. During these calls we will talk briefly about the clients' goals and about the level of assets they are interested in investing. I also ask that they send me copies of their financial statements. The purpose of requesting their statements is to prepare properly for our first meeting. I will then prepare an analysis of their current investments, in case they might have any questions concerning their portfolio.

The first meetings are simple and straightforward. Their sole purpose is for clients and I to learn as much about each other as possible. My goal in the first meetings is to truly understand clients' needs and goals. I want to hear all about them personally: their families, their occupations, their hobbies, and even their likes and dislikes.

We then fill out a client intake form, which addresses all of their personal financial data including: annual income, monthly savings, monthly expenditures, current assets, insurance products owned, and aspects of the estate. I will use this data to prepare personalized financial plans for our next meetings. I use the financial plans as communication tools that let my clients see exactly how they are situated in that moment and how we plan to help them get to their ultimate destination.

Early in the second meeting I ask this important question: "Have there been any major changes to your goals or financial situation since our last meeting?" I ask this question to clients because I am prepared to present recommendations to them and, if there has been anything life-changing, there is a possibility that my recommendations might need adjusting. If the answer is no, we proceed to review the clients' goals as they were stated in our first meetings. I'll address each of the goals individually, to confirm that this is exactly what they are looking to achieve.

I then move on to my recommendations. When I make my recommendations to my clients, I use as much support material as possible, along with the financial plan I have prepared. It is very important to me that clients thoroughly understand the investment, its benefits and its risk, and why it was chosen in relation to their goals.

After each recommendation, I give clients an opportunity to ask any questions they might have, as well as more probing Q and A from my end to make sure they understand the material we just reviewed. My ultimate goal for the second meeting is that clients will gain an understanding about why these individual investments were recommended (which is always to help them achieve their goals).

The third meeting takes place when clients have decided that they would like to move forward, or if they have additional questions they would like to have answered prior to moving forward. Asking additional questions is always good! I truly believe there are no stupid questions when it comes to your money.

Once clients give me the green light to move forward with my recommendations, we then start the process of moving their assets to my firm. My assistants and I always do our best to make sure the transfer and investment paperwork is a simple and easy process for clients. Once their funds hit the accounts at my firm, they are invested in the recommended products. I am truly blessed to have an excellent support staff, which ensure that the entire process is seamless and pleasurable for the client.

At this juncture, the second phase of my process, which is every bit as important as the first phase, kicks in. It centers on how clients and their accounts will be serviced throughout the course of the year. I believe it is important for an advisor to be able to clearly articulate exactly how he plans to deliver his service to clients. This should include scheduled meetings, either face-to-face or via the telephone. He should have a secondary point of contact as well, should a client need to contact the advisor before a scheduled meeting. You should want to make sure that the level of service that an advisor plans to deliver is acceptable to you.

Chapter Recap

- **Make sure that the initial process is done at a pace you are comfortable with.**

- **Understand exactly how your accounts will be serviced, not just from the outset, but also throughout the course of the year.**

Chapter 6

THE FINANCIAL PLAN

Last year, my good friend William was experiencing severe muscle cramps in his abdomen. He had never felt this sort of pain before, so he set up an appointment to see his doctor in two weeks. However, a few days later the pain worsened, so he drove himself to the nearest hospital and went to the Emergency Room. After a short wait, he was seen by a doctor who sent him to get an x-ray. After reading the results, the doctor examined him by probing his stomach area and asking a lot of questions. He prescribed a painkiller for my friend and scheduled him for an MRI the following week. The following week, William had the MRI done and, once the E.R. doctor was able to examine the results, he diagnosed him and prescribed the drugs William needed to get better.

It came time for Williams's appointment with his regular doctor. He decided to go, even though he was already being treated. When he arrived, he was surprised to find that his doctor had prescribed him medication based on the information William had left with the office assistant two weeks prior, when he had made the appointment. The medication the doctor had prescribed him was different from the medication the Emergency Room doctor had prescribed.

Which of the medications do you think William took? Which would you have taken?

When it comes to mapping out financial goals, it's safe to assume that everyone has at least one thing in common: a goal. However, that doesn't mean there is only one way to get there. Planning out someone's financial future is not a cookie cutter process, and there is no such thing as a "One Size Fits All" plan. I do not understand how people can take financial advice from anyone who has not taken the time to interview them to find out the details of their financial situations and their investment goals. That would be akin to William taking the medication which his doctor had prescribed him based on second-hand information that William told the secretary. Although he had just met the E.R. doctor, William followed his prescription instead of his regular doctor's. The E.R. doctor had taken the time to examine Williams' current situation. Likewise, it is very important that your financial advisor know your current financial situation, so that he or she can make the appropriate recommendations.

Put it in Writing

I always recommend that people work with a financial advisor who provides a written financial plan. I am amazed that I have yet to take on clients whose previous financial advisors provided them with a written financial plan. It hadn't mattered if the person was a retiree or pre-retiree, and regardless of the status of their income or asset level, none of my clients had ever been given a personalized plan in writing. This fact is shocking but true. The reality is that a large number of advisors do not use a true financial plan for their clients.

I think that there is a more practical and sound method of doing things, especially when you consider that the financial plan is useful not only to the client but to the advisor as well.

Think about it: would you ever consider taking a trip across the country, to somewhere you have never been before, without a map or a GPS system to show you exactly how to get to your final destination? Unfortunately, this is what most people do when planning for retirement if they work with a professional who doesn't provide them with a written financial plan. Make no mistake about it: simply recommending a portfolio of investments is not a financial plan! It falls well short of addressing many major concerns that most clients have.

Why in Writing?

A written plan clearly defines from the outset how you are financially constructed. It diminishes the chances that you will follow advice without understanding the amount of risk needed to achieve your goals. It clarifies the rationale for why you are being recommended certain investments.

Also, when you have your annual review with your financial advisor, the written plan will clearly show where you were when you began and what progress you have made towards your goals. It gives your advisor and yourself a vantage point from which you can see if you should keep your present course or if you should consider different options. It is important that you are not only on the right trajectory in the accumulation phase of the process but that you are on pace to reach your goals.

Financial Planning Software Tools

Today there are financial planning software options that help advisors tremendously in the planning process. On the whole, they are designed to address a wide variety of client concerns: current and future income needs, social security, future healthcare needs, taxation, legacy, household budgets, savings, shortfalls, surplus projections, insurance and more. I recommend that your financial advisor be adept at utilizing software tools such as these, so that he will be well equipped to meet his clients' needs.

As I mentioned previously, the financial plan is a very useful tool for both the client and the advisor when starting out their new relationship. The priority for the financial advisor in that first meeting with you should be to gather as much information about you as possible. If the advisor is using financial planning software, a substantial amount of information has to be entered about you – which, again, can help your advisor be more thorough in his process and provide consummate service to you. If done correctly, it should become apparent to your advisor what recommendations to suggest. Without this initial process, I would find it nearly impossible to make the proper recommendations to my clients.

Chapter Recap:

• Look to work with a financial advisor who provided clients with a financial plan.

• If a financial advisor is not using a financial planning software, he should be!

Chapter 7

BIG BANK ADVISOR VS. INDEPENDENT ADVISOR

Multimedia has enabled financial firms to become household names with which we are all familiar. I'm sure these days even most children could name at least a couple of firms. Internet surfers, television viewers and radio listeners are constantly bombarded with commercials from a litany of investment firms. Yes, I am guilty of this as well. I advertise on the television and radio year round to help build my brand.

The question is: how do you choose? The firms all seem reputable in their ads. They all do the same things, don't they?

There seems to be a ton of independents out there, too. You most likely know someone who has opened up an independent firm. He's the friend of a friend; you should give him a call, right? There can't be that much difference between a big name firm and an independent, can there?

If you happen to be in the position where you need to find a financial advisor, I know your quandary. With the big firm names constantly in front of you and your friend wanting you to meet John Doe, the independent, how can you tell who is right for you? After all, it's *your* hard-earned money, so you want to make sure you are going to have enough information to make the right decision.

One of the first tips I would give anyone is not to focus on the name brand (for whom the advisor may or may not work with). The truth of the matter is that while the aforementioned firms are most likely very fine institutions, keep in mind that you are not doing business with the institution, or the person in the commercial, or a trading software. You are doing business with an individual. With that in mind, focus on what is important so that you don't get blinded by a brand. You should base your decision on the individual and what he or she can offer you. It still doesn't make your decision easy, but it does make it more manageable. Understand that you are doing business with your advisor and not his brand.

What the general investing populace doesn't seem to consider when choosing their advisors is that these individuals also had a choice about how to conduct their business. Each advisor had to decide for him or herself whether to align with a big firm (and if so, which one) or to become an independent advisor. We, as advisors, must consider the resources of each firm for our clients and ourselves. We need to understand how the firm is going to help us in our practice, and how it can position us to provide the greatest options for our clients.

For me this was an easy decision.

I began my career with a big-name wire house that had, and still has, a great reputation. This firm shared its name with a major investment company that I am sure you would instantly recognize. My overall experience there was very positive. The office was managed well, the investment options appeared diverse, and the support staff was solid. I truly had no complaints with that institution.

What I found interesting during my time there was how prospective clients either loved or hated the fact that I worked for a major firm. It can be a very polarizing issue for people, when it comes to the management of their assets. What I quickly realized was that most clients were more comfortable with getting advice from someone without the influence of a parent company, someone who deemed diverse investment options important.

It was a very easy decision for me to become an independent advisor. I never considered it a risky move whatsoever. My clients had made it clear that they wanted things I was unable to provide at the big firm at the time. However, as an independent I was able to offer investments and recommendations that I could not have before, since there were no longer any strategic company partnerships getting in the way.

As an independent, my recommendations became more diversified, and my business began to grow quickly. The clients I started working for began to recommend me in earnest to their circle of peers, which I truly appreciated. Becoming independent allowed my clients to have greater confidence that I worked for them and their best interests, not a bank's best interest.

Have you ever been to a party at a great restaurant where, in order to expedite the food so as to serve hundreds of people in a short amount of time, the menu has been limited? I went to a wedding once where the bride and groom had rented out the entire restaurant, but the attendees could only select from four main dishes. The food was every bit as good as from the normal menu, yet I would have liked to have seen the normal menu. There might have been a dish I would have preferred.

When I was working for a big name firm, I felt as if I had to limit my 'menu' for my clients. Sure, the food (investments) was still good, but I wished I could have offered my clients more, given them a wider selection. As an independent, I feel that by being able to offer more options than before, I am of better service to my clients.

I have been independent now for quite a while, and things have definitely changed in my industry for the better. The big firms and the independent firms are now very similar: they offer almost identical options across the board. I tell you this because I want you to understand that you really should center your choice on the individual advisor. At the end of the day, the clients who came on board with me then and who come on board with me now do so for the same reason. They trust the relationship that I have been able to build with them through my expertise, honesty, and clarity.

I recommend that your next advisor have those three qualities. If so, it doesn't matter much if the advisor works at a big name firm or is independent. Just make sure he or she possesses those qualities.

Chapter Recap:

- **Remember that you'll be doing business with an individual and not a name brand.**

- **A firm's name should not be a major factor in your decision-making process.**

Chapter 8

RESOURCES MATTER

If you were looking to contract someone to build you your dream home, what would you look for? Most likely, you would prefer to find a company that could handle everything in-house. I mean, you wouldn't trust one of those "I got a guy" people, would you? They may be well connected to people in several areas of construction, but they work by themselves. Typically, their answer to something that they can't do starts off with "I got a guy…"

The problems, of course, with contracting someone like that are:

What if something happens to his "guy"?
Who exactly would be managing the project?
Would you have to interact with seven different people?

For me, I find it better to hire a construction company that has all of the resources under the one roof. You have one person managing the building of your home, and that person has control over the workers, the materials and the schedules.

In a sense, building a home is much like building an investment portfolio. A lot goes on behind the scenes of the financial advisor's office once you leave. There are money managers, compliance departments, and other people who work hard to build you your dynamic portfolio. The fact that he has everything at his disposal under one roof means that you only need to interact with him, and yet many qualified professionals are working on your behalf. Professional advisors like myself have an arsenal of resources. It gives us the flexibility and the wherewithal to build portfolios to address any individual's goals, like that builder who has masons, carpenters, roofers, tile guys, architects and painters, all on staff.

I will reiterate that it is important to know that you will be doing business with an individual and not a firm, or its brand. This chapter is dedicated to you understanding that the individual you decide to work with can only allocate you the resources at his disposal. When the right resources are available to your advisor, it can enhance the level of service and investment options you receive.

When I left the big-name brokerage firm, I had some tough choices to make. It wasn't easy for me to find out which firm was going to be the right fit for me. I needed a firm that would allow me to take my business to the next level by providing a better service experience for my clients.

I consider myself blessed to have discovered Independent Financial Partners. They are a regional firm that offered everything I was looking for and more. I was pleased to find out that IFP offers many great resources, including a money management division with several CFAs on staff, as well as a large, solid and responsive support staff. Even more appealing to me, their office location could not have been any better: it was centrally located between the three cities where the bulk of my clients reside.

Since joining IFP, my independent firm has grown exponentially, and the resources have as well. IFP has added an insurance division managed by seasoned veterans who are always willing to assist in case design. We also have a top-notch legal team and compliance department. Because of my surroundings, I have been able to take my business to the next level.

These resources have allowed me to provide an exceptional level of service to my clients, which has resulted in me getting the highest rate of referrals I've ever had in my career. I could not imagine being able to accomplish what I have accomplished in my practice without these resources being available to me. I was fortunate to have selected the right firm, not only for me but for my clients.

The reason I was able to find the right firm? It was because I went through the same process that I am asking you to go through when selecting your financial advisor.

Chapter Recap:

- **Resources matter, so find out what resources are available to your advisor.**

Chapter 9

HEART OF A TEACHER

t is not uncommon for us to admire famous people such as actors, athletes or artists. It's also not uncommon for people in business to admire very affluent individuals who have created empires, such as the Bill Gates' of the world. While I can certainly appreciate those people that rise to the top of their professions, when I get up to go to work, I'm not thinking of becoming The Donald. I don't have anything against him; it's just that I aspire to be more like someone else, someone like Dorina Sackman. Have you heard of her?

Miss Sackman recently won the Florida Department of Education/Macy's Teacher of the Year 2014! The most interesting thing about Dorina winning the Teacher of the Year award is that she teaches English for Speakers of Other Languages (ESOL), and she doesn't always teach the same kids throughout a school year. She educates children from other countries who speak a different language. She teaches them not only the English language but how to be themselves and flourish in the American school system. So how did someone who bounces around, teaching kids from the third grade on up to high school seniors, beat out every other teacher in the state of Florida to become the Teacher of the Year 2014?

She truly has the heart of a teacher.

Another person I greatly admire, radio host and author Dave Ramsay, also advises you to find an advisor who has the heart of a teacher. He recommends you search until you find that special someone with an ability to communicate things that, at times, are fairly complex. He would know better than just about anyone else that part of educating a client is a vetting process. At the end of the day, it's your job to know what you are spending your money on. (Here's a hint: if you can't articulate it yourself, someone didn't inform you well enough.)

When I give a recommendation to a client, I make sure that they understand everything I recommend to them. I will even go as far as having question and answer breaks throughout the recommendation process during which the client demonstrates to me his or her complete understanding of the investment. At times I can be guilty of over-educating, but I feel that it is imperative for my clients to fully understand the risk vs. the reward and how each individual investment fits into their ultimate game plan.

I have had countless new clients come to me after working with other advisors, and yet they have absolutely no understanding of their investments. This always amazes me, no matter how many times I come across this scenario, which unfortunately happens quite often. After going through my recommendation process, wherein I take the time to educate about my recommendations, my clients tend to become much more engaged investors.

It has been my experience that engaged investors are successful investors. Simply stated, I believe people do what they like to do and can understand, but they avoid doing things they are not good at or don't understand. Here's a good example: if you are an excellent golfer, you will most likely enjoy playing a lot of golf; if you don't play well you will probably avoid the sport entirely. I believe investing is a lot like golf in this way. If you don't understand your investments, you most likely will not feel comfortable with your investing, and thus not become an engaged investor.

Back when I was in college, I had to sign up for Organic Chemistry, of all things. What college kid wants that class? I went to the first class convinced that it was going to be the worst experience of my college career, but then I met Dr. Goldberg. Wow, that man could teach! He had such a passion for organic chemistry, and he explained very complex matters with such ease and grace that it became my favorite class. I hope you can also recall a teacher who made a positive impact on you. For me, it was Dr. Goldberg.

One thing about Dr. Goldberg that stands out in my memory is that, whenever a student would raise a hand to ask a question, the professor would always take the time to thoroughly answer the question. He also delivered the information in a way that made it easier for the student to grasp. It was obvious that he knew how important it was to go the extra mile with every question. When I look back now, I realize that he really wanted his students to understand what he was teaching them. It showed in his enthusiastic approach. It was evident that he was always eager to educate, unlike some other college professors I had who would sigh loudly whenever someone raised a hand, as if it were a burden to answer the question. On occasion I have even seen college professors belittling students for asking what they perceived to be 'silly questions.' Imagine hiring a financial advisor responsible for your investments who has that attitude toward you when you ask questions? Dr. Goldberg truly had the heart of teacher. In my opinion, so do the best financial advisors.

If you are reading this book, I want to give you an A for understanding that it is important to hire a professional to assist you with your investments. I suggest finding an advisor who is passionate about educating clients. You should be able to tell in your first or second meeting if your advisor has the heart of a teacher. I salute the Bill Gates' and the Warren Buffets' of the world, but I reserve my standing ovations for people like Dorina Sackman and Dr. Goldberg. They have the heart to teach. Your financial advisor should too.

Chapter Recap

- **Look for a financial advisor that enjoys educating his clients.**

- **Engaged investors are successful investors.**

Chapter 10

GO WITH YOUR GUT!

First and foremost, I am a firm believer in doing business with people I know, like, and trust. A quality referral is by far the best barometer when choosing a financial advisor. The fact is, without a referral from someone you know and trust, you will not have the luxury of knowing much in advance about the advisor you are about to select. I suggest you do your due diligence. Go through the checklist I have provided in this book.

Once you have gone through the list, however, you may find that you have more than one option. This is when your intuition, your gut, kicks in.

Know Thyself

Ultimately, I believe that knowing who you are and being comfortable with yourself is the first step to becoming a secure and confident person. Only you know the types of business relationships that have worked well for you in the past and the ones you wished you had a time machine to erase. Although our spouses may tend to think that they know us better than we know ourselves (and even order the food they think we are going to want at times), the reality is that they don't know when we are in the mood for seafood or steak unless we tell them. Only you truly know you!

Once you know who you are, you discover what your preferences are. Then you acquire a basis for determining what type of relationships you want. In terms of finding the right financial advisor for you, you may prefer to have one that tells great stories and makes you laugh, or you might like the no-nonsense, strictly business type. No one can tell you which advisor is the one that you will be happy with a few years down the road. After you have gone through the process of due diligence, only your gut can tell you.

Some of the best professional athletes have learned to play their sport instinctively. They no longer have to make quick decisions while playing the game. They trust their instincts, and so they are quicker to react. At times they know where the play is going before it gets there. They react before their eyes and brains tell them to. We all have that intuition: it's called *a gut feeling* In simple terms, it means to trust your feelings when deciding what to do.

After you have done your due diligence in pre-screening your next financial advisor, make sure that you interview him or her. You can always tell when you meet true professionals; there is a certain aura about them. All the pieces fit. Once you have the opportunity to meet in person with the advisor, it usually becomes obvious pretty quickly if it's the real deal or not. Throughout your conversation the advisor will say things that will either build your confidence or raise red flags.

The more questions you ask, the better. Remember that other old saying that has been around for a long time because of its value: *there is no such thing as a silly question* (to which I would add, especially when it comes to your money). The more you interact with your advisor, the more the insights to which you will be privileged.

Intuition

Aside from being a financial planner, my wife and I are involved in investing in real estate. We recently looked at a particular property, a condo in a high-rise building. It was priced substantially below market value. We figured there must have been a good reason for the low price. However, being that it was in an extremely attractive area, we figured it might be worth our time to check it out. Once we saw it, we fell in love with it. We knew we would be putting only a minimal amount of money into getting the property back in shape. We estimated that it would take approximately nine months for us to get a good return on our investment and time.

We put in a decent offer, and we felt good about it. We began our process of getting the property updated and ready. I contacted the contractors we normally use. I couldn't have been happier about the diamond in the rough we had found.

However, during the 10-day inspection period my wife started to get a bad feeling about it. We have been together long enough for me to respect and trust her intuition, just as she has learned to respect my opinions as well. She told me her gut was telling her that there was a lot more to the property than we knew. She would still move ahead with it if I wanted to, but she advised that we proceed with caution.

Taking her intuition into account, we decided to speak with other tenants in the building. When we spoke with the kind folks who lived below the condo for which we had made the offer, we saw that they were in the process of renovating their condo. It turned out that they had experienced water damage a few months prior. When they went about getting it fixed, they found extensive mold in the walls of their habitation—caused by the condo that we were looking to buy! Obviously, we rescinded our offer and ran out of there as fast as we could.

The point of this story is that, had we not believed in gut feelings or intuition we would have made a big mistake. It could have cost us hundreds of thousands of dollars and a large amount of time!

If you examine your own life, you might remember many times when you had a bad feeling about something. Either you chose to change your course to avert disaster, or you disregarded the intuition and later wished you had adhered to it. Again, when it comes to selecting the right financial advisor for you, there is a process written in this book that I strongly recommend you go through. Once you have finished, look inward and trust your gut.

Then and only then will you have given yourself the best opportunity to reach your financial goals.

I hope that this book has been an entertaining and informative read for you. More importantly, I hope it has helped you establish parameters for how to select a financial advisor that will be a good fit for you and your family. I believe that having the right financial advisor is every bit as important as having the right doctor.

Chapter Recap:

- **Do your due diligence: do your research. If at the end you are left with a list of qualified names, go with your gut!**

ACKNOWLEDGEMENTS

Thank you to Erin Tamberella from Executive Transformations Inc. Your timely counsel kept me from straying down rabbit holes. You were there to support me with this project, and you gave me some insightful tips on how to maximize my efforts.

I would also like to thank Eli Gonzalez, The Ghost from The Ghost Publishing. It was a pleasure to work with such a talented and creative person. You are a phenomenal writer. Not only that, but you are a consummate professional. I enjoyed every step of the collaboration process in getting this book written and published.

Securities offered through LPL Financial. Member FINRA/SIPC. Investment advice offered through Independent Financial Partners (IFP), a registered investment advisor and separate entity from LPL Financial.

ACKNOWLEDGMENTS

www.ingramcontent.com/pod-product-compliance
Lightning Source LLC
Chambersburg PA
CBHW071812170526
45167CB00003B/1275

9 781498 416368